P9-CMU-054

The Glace Bay Miners' Museum

A Play Based on the Novel by Sheldon Currie

The Glace Bay Miners' Museum

A Play Based on the Novel
by Sheldon Currie

Wendy Lill

Talonbooks
1996

Copyright © 1996 Wendy Lill

Published with the assistance of the Canada Council.

Talonbooks
#104—3100 Production Way
Burnaby, B.C., Canada, V5A 4R4

Typeset in New Baskerville and printed and bound in
Canada by Hignell Printing Ltd.

Second Printing: August 1998

No part of this book, covered by the copyright hereon, may
be reproduced or used in any form or by any means—graph-
ic, electronic or mechanical—without prior permission of
the publisher, except for excerpts in a review. Any request
for photocopying of any part of this book shall be directed
in writing to CANCOPY (Canadian Copyright Licensing
Agency), 6 Adelaide Street East, Suite 900, Toronto, Ontario,
Canada, M5C 1H6, Tel.: (416)868-1620; Fax: (416)868-1621.
Rights to produce *The Glace Bay Miners' Museum: A Stage
Play Based on the Novel by Sheldon Currie*, in whole or in
part, in any medium by any group, amateur or professional,
are retained by the author. Interested persons are requested
to apply to her agent: Patricia Ney, Christopher Banks
Agency, 6 Adelaide St. E.t, Suite 610, Toronto, Ontario,
Canada M5C 1H6; Tel.:(416)214-1155; Fax: (416)214-1150.

Canadian Cataloguing in Publication Data

Lill, Wendy, 1950—
  The Glace Bay Miners' Museum

  ISBN 0-88922-369-6

  I.Title. II.Currie, Sheldon. The Glace Bay Miners' Museum.
PS8573.I429G53 1996   C812'.54   C96-910515-0
PR9199.3.L517G53 1996

The Glace Bay Miners' Museum was first co-produced by Eastern Front Theatre and Ship's Company Theatre in August, 1995 at Ship's Company Theatre in Parrsboro Nova Scotia and subsequently at The Sir James Dunn Theatre in Halifax in September. The cast was:

MARGARET..Mary Colin-Chisolm
GRANDPA ....Peter Elliott
CATHERINE ....Niki Lipman
IAN..Ross Manson
NEIL..Hugh Thompson

Director...Mary Vingoe
Set Design...Stephen Britton Osler
Lighting Design ....Michael Fuller
Costume Design.................................Gay Hauser
Composer..Paul Cram
Stage Manager....................................Johanne Pomrenski

A shortened version of *The Glace Bay Miners' Museum* was produced for CBC Radio in 1991, directed by Paula Danckert.

Acknowledgements:

Many people have been involved in bringing this play to the stage; Mary Vingoe, my artistic director and co-conspirator in many important things, the original cast of the production who worked with dedication on this material right up to the last minute to make it the very best it could be, Paula Danckert, for helping to shape much of it for radio, and most important, Sheldon Currie, for writing the jewel of a short story of the same name many years ago. Working with such a generous and gracious storyteller has restored my faith in the power of stories to reinvigorate the world. Thank you Sheldon.

"Margaret, are you grieving?"

from Spring and Fall
by Gerald Manley Hopkins

CHARACTERS:

Margaret MacNeil

Catherine MacNeil

Ian MacNeil

Grandpa

Neil Currie

SETTING:

Glace Bay, Cape Breton

The Glace Bay Miners' Museum is a memory play.

ACT ONE
Scene One

A house on the ocean near Glace Bay, Cape Breton Island. There is the sound of waves slapping softly at the shore. MARGARET is looking out the window over the ocean. She begins singing a Gaelic air.

MARGARET:
Suilean dubha dubha dubh
Suilean dubh aig m'eudail
Suilean dubha dubha dubh
Cuin' a thig thu cheilidh

MARGARET switches to a bawdy Cape Breton ditty.

Balls to yer partner back against the wall
If you can't get shagged on Saturday night
You'll never get shagged at all!

She stops singing and goes over to a table and picks up a teapot.

Here is the teapot from the house at Reserve. Here is the teapot that steeped the tea that went down the hatch and warmed the guts of all the poor buggers that went down the hole at the Glace Bay mines. God bless them all. And over there, are their cans and their lamps, their boots and the likes... More in the other room. And while you're in there take a minute to stop at the window and look out— If it weren't for that little stretch of water out there you could see right clear over to the Isle of Skye.

That's what Neil used to say. Just take a look around. Don't be shy. There's lots to see. Look and ye shall see.

MARGARET sings a bit more.

The first time I ever saw the bugger, I thought to myself, him as big as he is, me as small as I felt, if he was astraddle on the road, naked, I could walk under him without a hair touching. That's what I thought. I was sitting alone at the White Rose Cafe wishing my girlfriend Marie would come by but knowing she wouldn't. None of the boys would sit with me and none of the girls either 'cause the boys wouldn't. For one thing, I had a runny nose. If a boy walked home with me, they'd say things like "I see you're taking out snot-face these days. Don't forget to kiss her on the back of her head." The other reason no one would sit with me was because I screwed a couple of boys when I was little. I didn't know you weren't supposed to and I didn't REALLY screw either of them 'cause they didn't know how to do it and it was too late before I could tell them, although, God knows, I knew little enough myself of the little there is to know. They didn't walk home with me after. Neither one. But they told everybody I was a whore. So I was not only a whore, but a snot-nosed whore. Marie was the only one who didn't care about any of that stuff and when she wasn't around to talk to I spent a lot of time staring at my little hands.

The sounds of the White Rose Cafe begin. Dishes clacking, voices, silverware. MARGARET is now 21. It is 1947.

WAITRESS:
   (offstage) Two chips and eggs, over easy...coffee...

MARGARET:

So, I was sitting alone in the last booth at the White
Rose Cafe right by the kitchen and the washroom
when this giant of a man with a box in his hand
came bearing down the aisle looking left and right
and he kept on coming 'til he got to my booth and
saw there was nobody there but me with my lovely
long hair. When he stood there holding his box,
before he said anything, I thought to myself I wish
he'd pick me up and put me in his shirt pocket.

NEIL:

Can I put this here on your table?

MARGARET:

Suit yourself.

NEIL:

Can I sit down then?

MARGARET:

Suit yourself again.

NEIL:

Alright, I will.

> *NEIL places the box on the table, eases himself into the booth.
> He lays his hands out in front of him. MARGARET squirms
> about, trying to avoid his gaze and his knees beneath the table.*

NEIL:

That your knee?

MARGARET:

Yeh. Where d'you think I keep them when I'm
sitting down?

> *NEIL laughs.*

NEIL:
Do you want something?

MARGARET:
I already had something.

NEIL:
Would you like something else?

MARGARET:
I don't have any more money.

NEIL:
I'd like to buy you a bite to eat if you don't mind.

MARGARET:
Why?

NEIL:
You still look like you're a bit hungry. What do you want?

MARGARET:
I'll have a cup of tea and an order of chips.

NEIL:
I'll have the same.

NEIL looks around.

MARGARET:
She's over there having a smoke.

When NEIL turns to get the attention of the waitress, MARGARET grabs the metal napkin dispenser and inspects her face, wipes some dirt from her cheek and tries to tidy her hair.

NEIL:
(calls) Two orders of chips and tea please.

Then he turns back and looks at MARGARET.

WAITRESS:
(hollers order out offstage) Two orders of chips and tea
for snot-nose and her friend.

MARGARET embarrassed, coughs to mask the
waitress's remark. NEIL has had a few to drink. He
begins singing low a Gaelic song then breaks off.

NEIL:
You like that song?

MARGARET:
(offhand) It's alright.

MARGARET jumps up, comes back with the food.
She lays out the plates and the tea, nervously. NEIL
watches her.

MARGARET:
Pass me that ketchup. Please.

NEIL passes it.

MARGARET:
Thank you. Will you pass the sugar too. Please.

NEIL passes it, still watching her. MARGARET stirs
her tea.

MARGARET:
So why are you looking at me? Haven't you ever
seen a girl with a runny nose before?

NEIL:
Not since my sister. Makes me feel right at home.

MARGARET:
Is that so?

MARGARET watches in wonder as he throws back his head and laughs. Then he looks back at her.

NEIL:
Yeh. That's so. So what do you think?

MARGARET:
I think you're the biggest son of a bitch I ever saw.

NEIL:
Know what I think?

MARGARET:
What?

NEIL:
I think you're the smallest son of a bitch I ever saw. And all of this rain, what do you think of that?

MARGARET:
I don't mind it. Kind of like it.

NEIL:
And the fog?

MARGARET:
That too. It's kind of cozy.

NEIL:
Yes it is. Do you come here often?

MARGARET:
> Every week at this same exact time. After I finish cleaning MacDonald's house.

NEIL:
> And what's your name?

MARGARET:
> Margaret MacNeil.

NEIL:
> Well now, Miss MacNeil, it's been a pleasure meeting you. Perhaps we'll meet again.

MARGARET:
> Suit yourself.

NEIL:
> Okay, I will. My name is Neil Currie.

> *NEIL gets up to leave. MARGARET doesn't want him to.*

MARGARET:
> So what have you got in that big ugly box?

NEIL:
> Let me show you.

> *NEIL opens the box and proudly inspects the parts of a set of bagpipes. MARGARET stares at them.*

MARGARET:
> What in God's earth is that?

NEIL:
> *(amazed)* You've never seen bagpipes before!

MARGARET:
> Sure I have.

NEIL:
> Then what are these? *(he holds up the pipes)*

MARGARET:
> A bunch of brown sticks.

NEIL:
> And this?

MARGARET:
> It's a stupid looking plaid bag!

NEIL:
> You've never clapped your eyes on bagpipes! I can tell by that stunned look on your face!

MARGARET:
> Drop dead!

NEIL:
> Your name's Margaret MacNeil and you've never seen a set of pipes!

MARGARET:
> And I sure haven't missed them...so get out of here and leave me in alone!

NEIL:
> I will not.

NEIL begins to assemble his bagpipes.

MARGARET:
> What the hell are you doing?

NEIL:

I'm putting it all together and then I'm going to play you a tune.

MARGARET:

(looks around uneasily) I don't know about that mister.

> *NEIL starts up the beginning snarls and squeals of the bagpipes. MARGARET covers her ears. NEIL starts to play.*

OWNER:

(offstage) Get that goddamn fiddle out of here!

NEIL:

(protests) Just a minute!

OWNER:

(offstage) No minute! Get out of here! Get out! Get out! Get out!

> *NEIL puts down the pipes, rolls up his sleeves to get ready to fight. MARGARET jumps up.*

MARGARET:

I wouldn't do it. He's big.

NEIL:

I'm ready!

> *NEIL bounds off in the direction of the kitchen. The sound of a struggle ensues.*

OWNER:

(offstage) And don't come back!

NEIL comes hurtling through the air towards MARGARET, lands in front of her.

MARGARET:
You silly bugger. Are you hurt?

NEIL:
My ears hurt and my pride's hurt. *(hollers towards the kitchen)* That's no way to treat a war hero!

MARGARET:
(helping him up) Some hero.

NEIL:
(mutters) One thing I thought a Chinaman would never have the nerve to do is criticize another man's music!

MARGARET:
That's not music. That's what a cat sounds like when he gets his tail caught in the screen door.

NEIL:
That's no way for a MacNeil to be talking.

MARGARET:
Serves you right. Try standing up.

NEIL:
If I wasn't drunk, I'd give you my pipes to hold and I'd go back in there and get the shit kicked out of me again.

MARGARET:
Where do you live?

NEIL:
I have a room down on Brookside.

18

MARGARET:
Want me to walk you down?

NEIL:
Where do you live?

MARGARET:
Reserve.

NEIL:
You live with your father and mother?

MARGARET:
I live with my mother and grandfather. My father got killed in the pit. I gotta go. I need to get home before bingo. And my brother Ian too.

NEIL:
In a company house?

MARGARET:
In a two room shack my father built that you can't even turn around in. He said he had to work in the goddamn company mine but he didn't have to live in a goddamn company house with god-only-knows who in the next half.

NEIL:
Your father was right.

MARGARET:
My mom said he was too mean to pay the rent. But only when he wasn't around to hear it. Then he got killed.

NEIL:
I'll see you home. Sober me up. Perhaps you could make us some tea.

MARGARET:
Well, if you promise to keep that thing in the box.

MARGARET and NEIL exit.

Scene Two

Lights up on The Shack.

*IAN sits at the kitchen table reading the 'Glace Bay Gazette Steel Worker and Miner's News,' his boots and can in front of him. GRANDPA is playing darts, just missing CATHERINE as she walks by. CATHERINE is always straightening, always cleaning, obviously bothered by the **presence** of these two other beings in her space.*

CATHERINE:
> Where is that girl? Probably in a fight with somebody. I asked her to get me some thread and buttons. Where in the hell is she? Move your boots. Move your can. I'm trying to make tea for your grandpa before I get out of here.

IAN moves his boots but not his can.

CATHERINE:
> And move that too! Why doesn't your grand and glorious union get you lockers to put all your stuff in?

IAN:
> We have more important things to think about.

CATHERINE:
> Is that so?

GRANDPA scribbles something in his notebook, bangs his slipper on the table, shoves the notebook out into the air to no one in particular.

CATHERINE:
See what your grandfather wants.

IAN gets up and takes the scribbler, reads.

IAN:
"Where is my tea?"

CATHERINE:
Don't get your shirt in a knot. I'm doing my best.
Your father told me he'd build me a pantry but he
never got around to it. "Too busy talking to the
demerara." And Charlie Dave would've done it but
before he could put his mind to it, Maggie June
came along and had him building shelves in their
own little square yard of space. So, I never got my
pantry. It would have been nice to have it in time
for the wake. I remember every woman there trying
to cram in here to see what my kitchen looked like.
It was their big chance to finally get a look at one of
the shacks. Straining like a bunch of piglets to get
past their men and into my kitchen to see what I
could possibly have in here. But I held my head
high. It was clean. It served the purpose. The wife
of the mine manager, Mrs. MacDougall herself, said
you should have had it at the hall dear as if to say
to spare you the embarrassment—but I wasn't
embarrassed. I shot right back at her—"It does the
job. It was good enough for him to live in and it's
good enough for him to be dead in."

GRANDPA waves his scribbler about.

CATHERINE:
What now?

IAN takes the notebook, reads.

IAN:

"Did you pay the light bill?"

CATHERINE:

Yes, I paid it. I took my little pot of gold down to the office and paid it. And then their men... I'm convinced not one of them went to the toilet before he came. They had to use the outhouses of all our neighbours. They said they didn't mind but those that didn't have them sitting over old bootleg pits were worried they were going to get overfull. The honey man must have had quite the week of work after that wake.

GRANDPA writes something else, hands it to IAN.

IAN:

(reads) "Then turn on some lights."

CATHERINE turns on a light.

CATHERINE:

Is there anything else I can do for your highness?

GRANDPA scribbles something, hands it to IAN.

IAN:

"Your dress is ripped under the arm."

CATHERINE:

Well! Thank you for telling me. I'm waiting for Margaret to bring me some thread so I can fix it. Where is she? I'm going to miss the first card.

IAN:

She probably went into the movie to get out of the rain.

CATHERINE:
Well why don't you go see if you can find her?

IAN:
And what if I do? She won't come home with me. Probably make a big scene in the movie theatre. I don't need that.

CATHERINE:
He doesn't need that. I'll fix it when I can.

GRANDPA hands CATHERINE his notebook, she reads.

CATHERINE:
(reads) "You don't have to holler at me. I'm not deaf." I know you're not deaf. *(CATHERINE throws up her hands in exasperation)* How do I live in this place with the lot of you—him scribbling at me, her sliding around out there like a stray cat. And then there's you... with your head screwed on backwards.

IAN:
What do you mean?

CATHERINE:
I cleaned the MacDougall's house yesterday. Minnie was sick so I did it for her as well as my own. Well it's quite the place. Were you ever in it? I bet the kitchen's as big as your Union hall. With an electric stove and an electric fridge and an electric toaster and an electric clock humming away—everything hums. And shiny. Everything is so shiny. How in God's name can you keep anything shiny?

IAN:
It's upwind from the pit.

CATHERINE:

I guess so. Everything matches everything else. The kitchen curtains are made of the same material as the oven mitts and the tea-cozy. And while I was taking all of that in, in walked your heartthrob Peggy, and wouldn't you know, she was wearing a dress of the same stuff. What do you make of it?

IAN:

I don't know. Maybe they got a big bolt of the stuff from the co-op.

CATHERINE:

That stuff didn't come from any co-op store. The colours are too bright. Minnie says it came from Montreal and that it costs a fortune.

IAN:

(getting up) I gotta go mom.

CATHERINE:

And do you think you would be able to afford the likes of that for her highness Peggy with what you make in the pit? Well you can't. Even if your union gets the raise—which it won't.

IAN:

We'll get the raise.

CATHERINE:

Even so it wouldn't be enough to buy what she's got.

IAN:

(irritated) For the love of Jesus, who's talking about buying bolts of cloth?

CATHERINE:
Who's taking out the mine manager's daughter?

IAN:
I walked her home from the dance. That's all.

CATHERINE:
You were down at Dominion beach with her all day
Saturday. Margaret told me.

IAN:
Margaret's a snitch.

CATHERINE:
You're either taking out the manager's daughter or
you're thick with the union. You're either one or
the other. Where is your head?

MARGARET and NEIL enter, soaking wet.
CATHERINE is visibly impressed with NEIL's size
and stature.

CATHERINE:
(sarcastic) Well thank you for coming!

MARGARET:
I'm not late. It's only two minutes to eight.

CATHERINE:
You got my thread?

MARGARET:
Oh God! I knew I forgot something!

CATHERINE:
What did I expect?

MARGARET:
I'm sorry.

CATHERINE:
Well sure you're sorry. And who have you dragged in from the rain?

MARGARET:
This is Neil, Neil Currie.

NEIL:
How do you do.

CATHERINE:
Where'd you find him?

MARGARET:
In the Bay.

CATHERINE:
He looks a bit rough.

MARGARET:
He got in a fight. I'm gonna clean him up.

CATHERINE:
You from the Bay?

NEIL:
No, I just came.

CATHERINE:
Where from?

NEIL:
St. Andrew's Channel.

CATHERINE:
Never heard of it. You working in the pit? You look like you could use a shovel.

NEIL:
I was. I started but they fired me.

IAN:
Why'd they fire you?

NEIL:
Well I wouldn't talk English to the foreman.

CATHERINE:
You an Eyetalian?

NEIL:
No, I was using the Gaelic. Like our ancestors.

IAN:
I heard about that.

NEIL:
What did you hear?

IAN:
Just yesterday, up at No. 10. I heard there was a guy down in Lingan bellowing at the top of his lungs. The word was he'd snapped...

NEIL:
I was the sanest one there.

IAN:
(studying him) Well I don't imagine you need to talk English to dig coal. If that's all it was about, I'll bring it up at the union meeting tonight.

NEIL:
Don't bother. I was going to quit anyway.

IAN:
How come?

NEIL:
I got no use for it.

IAN:
Is that so?

NEIL:
That's so. Burrowing underground is a good job for worms.

IAN:
Is that so?

NEIL:
And unions just trick poor suckers into thinking they got some say in things.

IAN:
Then why'd you bother going down to begin with?

NEIL:
Why'd you take your first drink? All your buddies were doing it. And I needed the money. I just got back from overseas.

CATHERINE:
(new respect) You're a vet.

NEIL:
That's right.

CATHERINE:
    Well it's a bloody disgrace. We sent you off to fight
    for a new world, a new heaven, a new earth and
    you're back and your choice is the pit or relief.

NEIL:
    I won't take relief.

CATHERINE:
    Get this man some tea Margie. And get him a pair
    of your father's pants.

MARGARET:
    You might as well keep them. They don't fit anyone
    else around here.

CATHERINE:
    Well, I'm going to bingo. Come on Ian or you'll be
    late for your meeting.

    *CATHERINE gestures towards GRANDPA who has
    fallen asleep.*

CATHERINE:
    Don't forget your ancestor over there Margie. I hit
    him about an hour ago.

MARGARET:
    Okay mom. Hope you win it.

CATHERINE:
    Me too.

    *CATHERINE and IAN leave. MARGARET gets a
    wet cloth, starts wiping NEIL's face.*

NEIL:
    Ouch!

MARGARET:
>Serves you right.

>*NEIL tries to pull her close to him. She pulls away.*

MARGARET:
>If you kept your hands to yourself, you wouldn't get in so much trouble.

NEIL:
>I know that. Wouldn't have as much fun either.

>*NEIL looks over at the sleeping GRANDPA.*

NEIL:
>What's the matter with him? Why do you have to thump him?

MARGARET:
>He's got something wrong with his lungs. Every hour or two he can't breathe and we have to pound him on the chest.

>*NEIL picks up one of GRANDPA's scribblers from the table, opens it.*

NEIL:
>*(reads)* Thump my chest. Dinner. Beer. Water. Piss Pot. Ask the priest to come. Time to go now father. I have to get me thump. No, Ian'll do it."

MARGARET:
>He doesn't talk. He used to talk but it hurt him to talk after he came home from the hospital with his lung problem so he just quit doing it. I don't know if it got better or not because he never tried again; same as he quit walking after he got out of breath once from it. He took to writing notes. I gotta go change my clothes.

31

MARGARET exits. Lights up on the tiny room next to the kitchen which MARGARET shares with her mother. She goes to the mirror, slaps on some of her mother's powder and lipstick, a brush through her hair.

NEIL:

So does the poor old fellow just sit here all day?

MARGARET:

No, he chases the girls down on Dominion beach. Of course he just sits there!

NEIL:

Does he ever go out?

MARGARET:

No. He hates sun. That's why the curtains are closed. After working in the pit so long, it hurt his eyes. He mostly just sleeps like the old tomcat.

NEIL:

(softly, looking at the sleeping old man) No wonder. Look at this place.

NEIL goes and opens up the windows. Light pours in. GRANDPA snorts, goes back to sleep.

NEIL:

Well old man, I guess you're it eh? This is where we got to.

MARGARET:

(calls out) What are you talking about?

NEIL:

Oh nothing. I'm just talking to myself.

NEIL looks closely at GRANDPA's scribblers.

NEIL:

Do you know that under all his scribbles are... it looks like someone's written a diary... some of it's in Gaelic. Looks like he's just written right over them.

MARGARET:

(calls out) That's probably what he did. They must have been his mother's. When he stopped talking, he probably just hauled them out.

NEIL:

I wouldn't mind reading them some time.

MARGARET:

(calls out) Help yourself. We use them for hotplates and for fly swatters.

> *NEIL opens his bagpipe case and starts assembling his bagpipes. MARGARET yanks off her dress and begins digging around in a drawer for something prettier. She picks out a dress, shakes out the wrinkles. NEIL begins to play. GRANDPA startles, starts to wake. MARGARET, with her dress half on, comes running out.*

MARGARET:

Are you out of your brain? I told you to leave that thing in the box.

> *She sticks her fingers over the bagpipe holes.*

NEIL:

What are you doing?

MARGARET:
    I'm plugging up the holes. You're making too much
    noise.

NEIL:
    Your dress is falling off.

    *MARGARET, embarrassed, finishes doing up her
    dress. She notices GRANDPA is awake. His breathing
    is heavy, laboured.*

MARGARET:
    You woke him up!

NEIL:
    So? It's time everybody woke up!

    *MARGARET goes over to GRANDPA, rearranges his
    blanket.*

MARGARET:
    Grandpa? You alright? Want your thump?

    GRANDPA shakes his head, scribbles in notebook.

NEIL:
    What does he want?

MARGARET:
    Probably wants you to clear right out.

    MARGARET looks at the notebook.

MARGARET:
    Well, Christ in harness!

NEIL:
    What did he write?

MARGARET:
>   *(reads)* "Tell him to play some more."

>   *NEIL laughs, goes over to GRANDPA and bows.*

NEIL:
>   I would be honoured to sir.

>   *NEIL plays a short happy tune. GRANDPA's head bobs along with it.*

NEIL:
>   So what does that sound like?

MARGARET:
>   Two happy hens fighting over a bean.

NEIL:
>   *(to GRANDPA)* Do you like that?

>   *GRANDPA nods.*

NEIL:
>   Do you know that tune?

>   *GRANDPA hesitates then nods again.*

NEIL:
>   I thought you would.

>   *NEIL starts to play again, this time a gentle soothing tune. GRANDPA slowly falls off to sleep again. MARGARET relaxes in a chair against the wall, her toes tapping. She closes her eyes, her body relaxing, her knees falling open. NEIL stops playing and comes over and leans down and kisses her. MARGARET puts her two feet up on his chest and tries to push him*

away but nothing happens. They remain there, his
chest against her feet, NEIL looking up her leg.

NEIL:
Did you know you got a hole in your underwear?

MARGARET:
Frig off.

NEIL:
What's the matter with you?

MARGARET:
With me? Just because you play that thing doesn't
mean you can jump me.

NEIL:
Well why not? You looked like you were ready.

NEIL runs his hand down MARGARET's leg.
MARGARET jumps up and away from him.

MARGARET:
Frig off!

NEIL:
Fair enough. I won't jump you 'til we're married.

MARGARET:
Married? Who'd marry you? You're nothing but a
goddamn Currie.

NEIL:
(laughs) And why wouldn't you marry a goddamn
Currie?

MARGARET:

> Because they come into your house, play a few
> snarls on their pipes and they think you'll marry
> them for that.

NEIL:

> I'll tell you what. I'll play for you every night until
> you think you're ready. I'll even make you a song of
> your own.

MARGARET:

> What kind of song?

NEIL:

> I don't know. We'll wait and see what I can make. I
> got to know more about you first.

MARGARET:

> I want a song a person can understand so I'll be
> sure what it's saying.

NEIL:

> Fair enough. I'll make you two. One to sing and
> one to guess at. What would you like for the singing
> one?

MARGARET:

> How should I know?

NEIL:

> Well, what's the happiest thing in your life or the
> saddest.

MARGARET:

> They're both the same. My brother. Not the one
> living here now. He's just someone to put up with
> along with everything else. I mean my older
> brother, Charlie Dave.

NEIL:
> What do you like about him?

MARGARET:
> He used to fight for me, wouldn't let anybody call me names. He could clean anybody's clock in Reserve.

NEIL:
> Where's he now?

MARGARET:
> He got killed in the pit with my father.

NEIL:
> How old was he?

MARGARET:
> 16.

NEIL:
> Jesus! He couldn't have been in the pit very long.

MARGARET:
> Not even a year. He started working with my grandfather just before he quit for his lungs. Then he started with my father. Then he got killed.

NEIL:
> Tell me more about him.

MARGARET:
> Why should I?

NEIL:
> 'Cause I'm gonna write a song about him.

MARGARET:

He was good in school but he got married so he had to go to work. They didn't even have the chance to have their baby.

NEIL:

What happened to his wife?

MARGARET:

What do you think happened to her? Nothing! She had the baby. A sweet baby. He's eight now. They live up in the Rows. In a company house. With her mother and her sister. *(MARGARET's voice breaks with emotion)* Now look what you've made me do. It's time for you to clear out. I'm tired of your questions and your racket. *(MARGARET blows her nose)* My mother knew it was going to happen.

NEIL:

How did she know?

MARGARET:

Women know! They just know. Now pack up your sticks and leave.

NEIL:

Okay I'll go. But I'll be back again and I'll play to you every night 'til you're ready.

MARGARET:

I won't hold my breath.

> *NEIL kisses MARGARET lightly on the lips. Then leaves.*

MARGARET:

(to audience) But I did hold my breath and I near died a happiness!

Scene Three

The next morning. Dawn. A rooster calls. The sound of bagpipes begins in the distance, coming closer. CATHERINE and MARGARET are asleep in the bedroom. IAN is in a bedroom offstage. GRANDPA is asleep in his chair. They all begin to stir.

CATHERINE:
> What in hell....

IAN comes stumbling out of his room.

IAN:
> *(semi-sleep)* What's happening? Has the roof caved in?

CATHERINE gets up, opens the curtain. First light shines in.

CATHERINE:
> For the love of God. Will you look at that.

IAN grabs his pants.

IAN:
> What is it? What time is it?

He joins her at the window.

IAN:
> Jesus Christ!

CATHERINE:
> Even the chickens are diving for cover. And he's got a string of kids running after him like he was the pied piper.

MARGARET:
And he's heading this way!

CATHERINE:
He must be nuts.

IAN:
Well he's not coming in here at this hour or any hour.

MARGARET:
And who are you to say?

IAN:
I pay the bills here.

MARGARET:
Oh yeah? Big deal, big talk, big head. You don't pay all the bills.

IAN:
That's right—you two pay for the tea.

CATHERINE:
Will you listen to that thing. He's making enough noise to raise the dead. I haven't heard those things since... (*CATHERINE turns, looks around*) Will you look at this place!

> *GRANDPA starts to bang his slipper in excitement.*
> *CATHERINE starts straightening things.*

IAN:
What's the matter with it?

MARGARET:
Where's my hairbrush?

IAN:

Why do you want your hairbrush?

MARGARET:

You never know. *(jokingly)* He might ask me to get married.

IAN:

(snorts derisively) Why would he want to marry a dog?

MARGARET:

Well I'd rather be a dog than a dog's arsehole which is what you are.

CATHERINE:

Stop it you two.

MARGARET:

Where is my hairbrush?

IAN:

A total stranger arrives at six in the morning playing the bagpipes and you're all...

GRANDPA bangs his slipper, points in the direction of her hairbrush. MARGARET goes over and kisses him, grabs her hairbrush. IAN sees the excitement in his grandfather's eyes.

IAN:

Oh for the love of God. You'd think the Messiah himself was about to arrive.

The sound of the bagpipes arrive at the door then stop. There's a knock. They all stand looking at it.

MARGARET:

He's here.

CATHERINE:
Well open it.

MARGARET opens it.

MARGARET:
Hello.

NEIL:
Good morning, Margaret. I've come for a visit.

NEIL pulls a bouquet of flowers from his pack, hands them to CATHERINE.

NEIL:
Some flowers for you, Mrs. MacNeil.

CATHERINE takes the flowers, speechless.

NEIL:
You look lovely this morning, Margaret.

MARGARET:
Thank you.

NEIL:
And good morning to you too, Ian.

Then NEIL goes over and takes off his cap to GRANDPA, shakes his hand.

NEIL:
And to you sir. A good morning.

GRANDPA waves his scribbler about eagerly.

NEIL:

(reads) "Do you know 'Guma slan to na ferriv chy harish achun'?" Yes I do, and I'll be glad to play that for you... if you'll pay me back with a story.

GRANDPA *hesitates, then nods.*

IAN:

So what do your parents do up there in that place... St. Andrew's Channel?

NEIL:

They're farmers.

IAN:

Is that so? What kind of farm?

NEIL:

They grow vegetables. They raise cattle.

MARGARET:

Sounds like something you'd like Ian. You're so fond of animals. He's been dragging poor animals home since he was this high. The weirder the better. Salamanders, turtles, snakes, bugs. I came in once and caught him kissing a mouse. Charlie Dave was out playing hockey and he was in here kissing mice.

IAN:

Oh stop your yapping.

MARGARET:

Mr. Kiss-a-mouse.

IAN:

Yap, yap, yap!

MARGARET:
 The next time I see Peggy I'm going to tell her you
 like kissing mice too.

CATHERINE:
 Tea, Margaret, tea!

IAN:
 So why didn't you go back there when the war
 ended?

NEIL:
 I wanted to but there wasn't any land left. I had
 seven brothers and two sisters.

IAN:
 The boys all farmers?

NEIL:
 Nope. One of them's a teacher. One of them's a
 doctor.

IAN:
 A doctor?

 IAN would have loved to have been a doctor.

NEIL:
 Three of us were mucking about in the war.

IAN:
 Three of you fought in the war?

NEIL:
 Two of us didn't come back.

MARGARET:
 Jesus!

CATHERINE:
Your poor mother. War is worse than the mines.

MARGARET:
The war'd be over before Ian ever got to it. He's got to know everything first?

CATHERINE:
Stop it Margie.

MARGARET:
And he's not a fighter anyways.

IAN:
Would you shut your mouth.

MARGARET:
Charlie Dave jumped at the chance of a fight. He woulda been there in a second if he could.

CATHERINE:
Oh for the love of God.

MARGARET:
Charlie Dave loved it when someone stole my mitts. Then he'd wade in and beat the shit right out of them. But not our Ian. He's a mouse kissing mama's boy.

IAN:
And you're a snot-nosed whore!

NEIL:
Wait a minute! You can't call her that!

IAN:
And you can get out of my house!

IAN and NEIL's fists go up and they start circling each other.

CATHERINE:
Now look what you've done.

MARGARET:
Isn't it exciting?

CATHERINE:
You nitwit.

MARGARET:
Come on mom. When was the last excitement we had around here?

CATHERINE:
I guess the wake.

> *GRANDPA bangs his shoe on the table, shoves a notebook at MARGARET.*

MARGARET:
What?

> *She reads, then grudgingly steps between IAN and NEIL.*

MARGARET:
Grandpa's got a story for you.

> *GRANDPA bangs his slipper again.*

MARGARET:
(reluctantly) Do you want to hear it?

NEIL:
Yes, I do.

MARGARET:
>There was this fellow worked in the pit named Spider MacDougall who only wanted to do two things in life—work in the pit and snare rabbits. Until one day, Madeline Boyd caught up with him on his trapline and taught him how to do something else. After they'd done it, he told her that he'd never heard of it before except with rabbits and dogs. They had fifteen kids after that.

NEIL:
>What happened to him?

MARGARET:
>Spider got so sick of the pit he went funny one night and burned down the Company store. They threw him in jail where he died.

NEIL:
>That's a sad story.

MARGARET:
>That's a true story.

>*NEIL puts down his fists. He nods to GRANDPA.*

NEIL:
>Thank you. *(then turns to IAN)* Look, I don't want to fight either Ian. Not with you. You seem like a smart fella. You obviously think a lot. I just want to visit here. I want to hear your grandfather's stories. I want to read his scribblers. Let's not use our fists on each other. It's a waste of energy. Is it a deal?

IAN:
>*(puts down his fists)* It's a deal.

NEIL:

D'you play cards?

IAN:

Yeh.

NEIL:

Do you drink rum?

IAN:

Sure.

NEIL pulls out a flask, passes it to IAN.

IAN:

It's only six o'clock.

NEIL:

D'you care?

IAN:

No.

They clear the table, sit down and start playing cards.

MARGARET:

(to audience) Then after that, he came back and
came back and came back and there was nothing
but noise. My mother took to going out every night
as soon as she saw the sight of his hat coming over
the hill. He'd play songs and I'd tell stories from
Grandpa and if Ian was around, I'd raze him about
Peggy, and Ian and Neil would argue the leg off an
iron pot, then we'd walk Ian to the pit, then go over
to the wharf and watch the seagulls swooping and
screeching like little air planes. That was what I
liked. The water. The sound of the waves. Neil
would laugh and say to me, there's hope for you yet.

Sounds of the sea.

NEIL:

Why are you so hard on your brother?

MARGARET:

Dunno. 'Cause he just stands there and takes it. It's none of your business.

NEIL:

And why does your mom play bingo all the time?

MARGARET:

I guess she likes it eh? Why do you drink rum all the time?

NEIL:

(laughs) I guess I like it eh? How do women know that their men are going to die?

MARGARET:

Jesus! Will you ease up. We've come to enjoy the evening.

NEIL:

You're right. Let's just skip rocks and smell the fishy air.

MARGARET:

The dogs were howling three nights in a row at the full moon. Those goddamn dogs, once one starts, they all start. That was the first thing that tipped her off.

NEIL:

(scornful) She knew because of the dogs barking?

MARGARET:
That's not all. It was in the cards...

NEIL:
(snorts derisively) In the cards?

MARGARET:
I was up at the underground manager's house helping mom with the housework the night it happened and I had a game of auction forty-five with the girls—me and Mary against Morag and Peggy.

NEIL:
(sarcastic) And you saw it in the cards!

MARGARET:
I didn't see it right away. First I thought I was lucky. All them shovels. The five, the king, the queen, the jack and the ten of spades, but then I remembered what my mother always said.

NEIL:
What was that?

MARGARET:
Spades mean death. Shovels dig the hole. The only thing can save you is a heart. A heart can block four shovels. Only hearts' desire can conquer, even death. I needed the ace of hearts. So I threw in my ten and dealt myself the card off the top—I couldn't believe my eyes.

NEIL:
What?

MARGARET:

It was the ace of spades. And then the sirens started
to wail.

NEIL:

Oh come on!

MARGARET:

It was in the cards!

NEIL:

That's just a bunch of malarkey!

MARGARET:

Then why are your eyes popping out like a scared
rabbit's?

NEIL:

Lets not talk about it anymore.

MARGARET:

(miffed) Fine. We'll just lie down here in the grass
and look at the stars.

They lie silently for awhile.

MARGARET:

What was it like over there in France?

NEIL:

Lots of pretty girls. Lots of cheap wine. I had the
time of my life.

MARGARET:

How come you went berserk that day down in the
shaft?

NEIL:

> (*sitting up*) I don't want to talk about that.

MARGARET:

> What about your brothers who didn't make it back?
> Were you together?

NEIL:

> Yeah. One minute they were smelling the air beside
> me and the next minute they weren't. I don't want
> to talk about that either.

MARGARET:

> (*after a pause*) My mother even told him not to go
> down that day. It was the last day of work before
> vacation. She told him if he spent that day in the
> garden and the next two weeks in the garden,
> instead of that day in the pit and the next two weeks
> drinking, then he'd have more money at the end of
> it, and vegetables to boot. And not rumsick at the
> end of it if not dead.

NEIL:

> Sounds like a man after my own heart.

MARGARET:

> I could hear the tears coming up in her throat. "If
> you don't go to the pit today, you won't get kilt in it,
> and I'll buy you the moonshine myself." That's what
> she said. "I'd rather have you dead drunk than
> dead." And he just stood there beside Charlie Dave.
> He'd come to pick him up. Just stood there with his
> lunch can under his arm and a smirk on his face.
> And he said, "You're my sweet little gyroch."

NEIL:

> (*laughs*) His sweet little pain in the ass.

MARGARET:

Is that what that means? She thought it was a pet name.

NEIL:

It is in a way. It's like a cow that gives a whole bucketful of beautiful creamy milk morning and night but every time with the last spurt, she puts her shitty hoof in it. What happened then?

MARGARET:

Then the two of them pursed their lips and lifted their hands like in a little wave... and they went out the door, and out the world altogether.

NEIL:

Go on.

MARGARET:

What do you mean, go on. They are dead! D.E.A.D.! Dead. There isn't anymore. She changed after that. All she does now is talk about the wake and go to bingo. I hate talking about the dead.

NEIL:

Then why do you do it all the time?

MARGARET:

Because you keep asking me! Why do you want to know all of this?

NEIL:

'Cause I'm going to marry you. I'm going to be part of the family.

MARGARET:

That'll be the day! I'll be living in that shack with my mom 'til the end of time!

NEIL:
    You'll be living with me.

MARGARET:
    Don't talk nonsense.

    NEIL starts kissing her neck.

NEIL:
    Alright. We won't talk at all.

    NEIL pushes MARGARET down on the grass and they start necking.

Scene Four

The Shack. GRANDPA is slumped over, spluttering and gasping for air. CATHERINE rushes in to the room.

CATHERINE:
Omigod!

CATHERINE pulls GRANDPA upright and positions herself so that she can give him a sound thump on the chest.

CATHERINE:
Christ in harness. That was a close one.

GRANDPA's breathing begins to return to normal. CATHERINE rubs his back.

CATHERINE:
I was just at the head of the road looking for her. It's way past midnight! How are you now? Is that better? (*GRANDPA nods*) Good. (*CATHERINE walks to the window, looks out*) What am I going to do with that girl? She's crazy for him. Mr. Neil Currie. He's a bit too sure of himself but he's got a fresh way about him and he's gentler then most of the scrappers she knocks about with. But she's so... unprotected. What's going to become of her? She's got about as much sense as a turnip.

GRANDPA hands her a scribbler. CATHERINE smiles, reads.

CATHERINE:
"And you had more?"

CATHERINE picks up a dishtowel and swats his shoulder.

Scene Five

Outside The Shack. NEIL is reading the diaries.
MARGARET is around and about. CATHERINE
walks out with a basket of laundry.

NEIL:

Listen to this. "1745, hardly half of them left alive.
Nineteen hundred ten and four, half in the pit and
half in the war." Your great-grandmother Morag
MacNeil was a bit of a poet.

CATHERINE:

She was a snarly old woman who never liked
anybody, especially me.

NEIL:

And why was that?

CATHERINE:

'Cause I snatched her favourite grandson out from
under her nose. She used to sit in the window of
her house spying on my every move.

NEIL:

It says here "Catherine Chisholm..." *(He looks up)* I
guess that was you eh? "Catherine Chisolm was the
liveliest spunkiest creature to ever grace our house.
She was like May after March. She was a jewel of a
girl for our Angus."

CATHERINE:

(astounded) Where does it say that?

NEIL:

Right here.

CATHERINE:
Let me see that!

CATHERINE takes the scribbler, looks.

CATHERINE:
Well I'll be damned. *(reads)* "A jewel of a girl for our Angus." Well I'll be damned! Who would have thought? *(reads)* "That lively lass was out there any minute she could grab riding around on her bike, playing peggy with those three dear children..."

MARGARET:
I remember that. You used to be a lot of fun.

CATHERINE:
Well I was hardly more than a kid myself. I wasn't about to sit around in the house all day listening to the old women. I hated being cooped up inside. So when did she write that?

NEIL:
(reads) "July 8, 1931. Sunny."

MARGARET:
Ian couldn't hold the bat without smacking someone.

CATHERINE:
Sports was not one of Ian's strengths. Isn't that incredible? And all those years, I thought that she thought... *(shakes her head)* Well, I'd better get going or I'll miss my bingo.

NEIL:
I thought you hated being cooped up inside.

CATHERINE:
I do.

NEIL:
Then why are you going off to sit in a smoky bingo
hall? Why don't we have a game?

CATHERINE:
Of what?

NEIL:
Peggy.

CATHERINE:
I'm too old for that.

NEIL:
That "lively lass," "that spunky creature."

CATHERINE:
That was nearly twenty years ago. I'm an old bag
now.

NEIL:
Tell that to the men downtown on Water Street.
Don't tell me you don't catch them looking at you.

CATHERINE:
Well they're all blind and half dead. They got pretty
low standards.

NEIL:
I bet Morag must have liked your sense of humour
too.

CATHERINE:
I'm too old to play peggy.

NEIL:
   No you're not.

MARGARET:
   C'mon mom.

CATHERINE:
   I don't play games.

NEIL:
   (to MARGARET) Go get your brother.

CATHERINE:
   This is foolish!

>   *NEIL marks out a circle out in the dirt with his boot.*
>   *MARGARET goes in the shack, interrupts IAN*
>   *reading the newspaper.*

IAN:
   What? What do you want?

MARGARET:
   We're going to play a game, egghead. C'mon.

IAN:
   What do you mean? A game?

MARGARET:
   A game. We're going to have some fun.

IAN:
   Jesus.

>   *GRANDPA grabs IAN's sleeve as he walks by.*

MARGARET:

>He wants to come. *(calls out to NEIL)* We need help
>with Grandpa.

>>*NEIL comes in.*

IAN:

>What's going on?

NEIL:

>We're going to play a game of peggy. *(to GRANDPA)*
>You can be the cheering section.

MARGARET:

>Some cheering section.

>>*NEIL and IAN carry GRANDPA in his chair outside
>>and put him down. NEIL pulls a picket from the
>>fence.*

MARGARET:

>Give it to me, I'll start. Pitch it to me.

IAN:

>I don't want to play.

MARGARET:

>You're pitiful Ian.

IAN:

>Oh give me the goddamned thing.

>>*IAN pitches it. MARGARET bats it. IAN tries to
>>catch it and misses.*

MARGARET:

>Butter fingers.

IAN:
>Snot-nose.

CATHERINE:
>Stop it you two.

MARGARET:
>Hope you know how to hold your own Peggy better than that.

CATHERINE:
>*(tries to stifle a laugh)* You stop that. It's none of your business Margie. My turn.

>>*CATHERINE gets up to bat and she blossoms. The years fall away. She hits it. GRANDPA claps, maybe even whistles.*

CATHERINE:
>I hit it! I hit it!

NEIL:
>Jeez you are good!

MARGARET:
>Way to go mom!

NEIL:
>It's your turn now Ian.

IAN:
>I don't wanna play this.

CATHERINE:
>Come on. Take a shot.

>>*Reluctantly, IAN takes the picket.*

MARGARET:
    This'll be a laugh.

NEIL:
    Let him concentrate.

MARGARET:
    Look at him. Pitiful. He can't fight. He can't sing.
    He can't hardly even hold a picket!

IAN:
    Trap up.

MARGARET:
    Charlie Dave used to hit it clear over the outhouse.

    IAN is getting more agitated.

MARGARET:
    What in the name of God does Peggy MacDougall
    see in you?

NEIL:
    Maybe she likes him for who he is and not for who
    he is not.

MARGARET:
    Well I guess that makes some sense but what the
    hell does it mean?

NEIL:
    It means that it's not his fault that he's alive and
    someone else is dead.

    NEIL pitches the peggy to IAN. He hits it.
    MARGARET tries to catch it but fumbles it.

IAN:
> (*surprised*) I hit it!

MARGARET:
> Well so you did. (*a new recognition here.*) Good shot
> Ian.

> *Note:*
> *The game of Peggy is a stick ball game played by*
> *people of French and Scottish descent in Eastern*
> *Canada.*

Scene Six

A half hour later. IAN and NEIL carry GRANDPA
back into the shack. CATHERINE sinks into her
chair, exhausted.

CATHERINE:
I'll pay for this in the morning.

NEIL:
It'll be worth it.

CATHERINE:
I'm going to bed.

MARGARET:
Don't go yet. Stay and have a hot one.

CATHERINE:
Just a little one. Might do some good.

MARGARET gets up and pours some rum and hot
water into a cup for her mother. GRANDPA bangs his
slipper, hands her a notebook on the way by.

MARGARET:
(reads) "Tell him about George Stepenak and Fergus
MacLeod."

NEIL:
Let's hear it.

MARGARET:
Do you think you could handle that Ian? You
worked with those guys.

IAN:
Oh, that was years ago...

65

MARGARET:
> So?

IAN:
> Well, I don't remember.

MARGARET:
> Well, Grandpa wants Neil to hear it.

IAN:
> Well God, let me see.... alright. There was this fella named George Stepenak and he was a Pole as you can tell by the name. I'm no good at telling stories.

NEIL:
> Go on.

IAN:
> Okay, so, he used to bring garlic in his can, and his can would stink and his breath would stink.

NEIL:
> Go on.

IAN:
> So, the men used to tease him all the time which made him cross and then one day Fergus said, "George, what in the name of Jesus have you got in that can?" "Shit," George said. And then I hear Fergus say, "I know that, but what did you put on it to make it smell so bad."
>
> *They all laugh. IAN is surprised and pleased with himself.*

MARGARET:
> *(turns to CATHERINE)* Why don't you tell us about when you met dad.

CATHERINE:
That's ancient history. No one wants to hear that.

GRANDPA bangs his slipper on the table, nods his head.

NEIL:
You're wrong Catherine.

CATHERINE:
Well, it was kind of.... well I was... and he was.... well it's not really very...

IAN:
Well spit it out!

CATHERINE:
(finally dives in) I met your father at the wake of Minnie's Uncle Joe Archie in the Bay. I was sneaking a smoke behind the outhouse. Your father knew I was there. He was two sheets to the wind, showing off for me, playing horseshoes and when the priest came up to tell him to stop, he said "I'll stop playing horseshoes if you'll stop squeezing the girls as they go by Joe Archie to pay their last respects. That probably offends him more than what I'm doing!" And when we were married two weeks later, you can bet, it wasn't that priest who tied the knot. We were in too much of a hurry for priests anyway. We went to a Justice of the Peace in Sydney. Can you imagine it? Nobody ever did the likes of that. When we came out of his office after the ceremony, there was a parade going by with a band of pipers. That was the last time I heard the bagpipes played—'til now. When we got home, somebody told Angus the priest was going to excommunicate him for what he'd done. And you know what Angus did? He marched right down to

the Glebe House and when the Father opened the
door, Angus said "You're too late. I excommunicated
myself last week." And he did. Never went back
there 'til the funeral. *(holds up her glass)* Cheers
Angus. I think I'll have another one of those hot
ones. *(CATHERINE laughs)*

NEIL:
You've got a beautiful laugh, Catherine MacNeil.

NEIL begins to play a reel with his bagpipes.

MARGARET:
(to audience) It was like the whole family was coming
out of hibernation after a long sleep. The music was
sweetening us up and firing us up. The rum would
come out and the cards would come out and every
Sunday afternoon, they'd take the world apart and
put it back together. Or fall over trying!

*IAN clears the table and brings out a deck of cards.
The flask of rum comes out.*

IAN:
The only hope, Neil-know-it-all-Currie, for the
miners in Cape Breton is to get a strong union.

NEIL:
Bullshit!

IAN:
If my father and brother had a strong union, they
wouldn't have died in that deathtrap.

NEIL:
Your father and brother should have stayed on the
surface of the world to begin with.

IAN:

Well they didn't and it's too late for that talk and it's
STILL a deathtrap 'cause the company doesn't
think they have to pay any attention to us. We need
a strong union to fight against those bullies.

NEIL:

Good men don't burrow in the ground like worms!

IAN:

That's what men here do. Good men!

NEIL:

Good men till the earth.

IAN:

Women have gardens here. Lots of women have
gardens.

NEIL:

Good men stand tall. They're king of their own hills.
They don't crawl around tunnels for a company or a
country that doesn't give a damn about them.

IAN:

You're full of shit.

CATHERINE:

You're both full of shit. The last man who had any
sense left here thirty years ago and went to Boston
and he's at least got buckles on his shoes.

NEIL:

The pit is death.

IAN:

Why do you say that? Look at me. I'm not dead.

NEIL:

I could feel it in my bones, the one time I went down there. It was the wrong place to be. I felt the same thing when I had my nose in the dirt staring through the sights of a gun over there in France. I saw death there and that's the truth.

IAN:

You got your head up your arse and you're facing backwards and that's the truth.

NEIL:

There is no future down there.

IAN:

There has to be a future.

NEIL:

See your grandfather? That's the future.

IAN:

Well he's there, isn't he? Don't knock my grandfather.

NEIL:

I'm not knocking your grandfather. I love your grandfather. But he can't breathe, he can't talk, he can't walk. You know the only thing he's got? Some old songs in his head that he can hardly remember, that your father hardly knew and you don't know at all. Came here and lost their tongues, their music, their songs. Everything but their shovels.

IAN:

Too bad you wouldn't lose yours. *(throws him the flask)* Have a drink and shut up.

NEIL:

I will not shut up. However, I will have a drink.

IAN:

> The only way to be strong is to be organized. We
> have to be strong as they are and then they'll
> negotiate. Now Neil, is that right or wrong?

NEIL:

> They'll send in the army.

IAN:

> Who?

NEIL:

> The government. They'll turn the boys against each
> other, the bastards. That's what they always do.

IAN:

> How do you know that's what they always do. You
> only been here two months.

NEIL:

> We've been here for a long long time, John.

IAN:

> My name's not John.

NEIL:

> Well now, John is English for Ian. I thought you
> might like it better. A union leader maybe should
> have a good English name.

IAN:

> I don't think I need you to tell me my name. I can
> remember my own name.

NEIL:

> Well what else to you remember John? Do you
> remember 1745?

IAN:

I guess nobody remembers 1745, eh?

NEIL:

Go and read your grandfather's scribblers John. He
remembers. His blood was spilled there, on the
ground, and our blood was spilled there, spilled on
the ground. He remembers. *(he opens up a scribbler,
pounds on it)* Look at this! *(reads)* "1745, hardly half of
them alive. Nineteen hundred ten and four, half in
the pit, half in the war." Look it's all there! Read it.

IAN:

I don't have time to read ancient history. I'm
working my ass off right here and now and that is
hellish hard enough.

NEIL:

Well if you don't have time to read it then go and
put your ear on your grandpa's chest, and listen to
his lungs singing, and maybe it will tickle your
memory. *(to MARGARET)* And what do you think
little mouse?

MARGARET:

(taking the bottle from him) I think that the square on
the long side of a triangle is equal to the sum of the
squares on the other two sides.

*NEIL laughs with delight. MARGARET leaves the
room. NEIL reaches over and retrieves the bottle.*

NEIL:

I don't think anybody could have put it any better.
So why don't we just play cards and have another
drink.

Scene Seven

Bedroom: CATHERINE is lying in bed. MARGARET enters. CATHERINE watches her brush her hair and undress.

CATHERINE:
That man'll never live in a company house. You'll be moving out of one shack and into another.

MARGARET:
I can stand it.

CATHERINE:
You can stand it. You can stand it. And is he going to work? Maybe Ian can get him on up at No. 10. He can work with Ian. Is that what you want? He's a rebel. He's a troublemaker.

MARGARET:
I can stand it.

CATHERINE:
You'll end up in another place just like this 'cause he's the way he is. And you're going to be the one who suffers.

MARGARET:
I can stand it mom.

CATHERINE:
Oh you can can you? They can die together, and you can stand it. And you can live in your shack alone. Stand it then.

MARGARET climbs into bed.

MARGARET:
    We're different.

CATHERINE:
    Sure.

MARGARET:
    I'm not you mom!

CATHERINE:
    Then who are you?

MARGARET:
    (*fierce*) Well I won't be you.

CATHERINE:
    You're young and stupid.

MARGARET:
    I'm glad of it.

CATHERINE:
    Don't ever say I didn't warn you.

MARGARET:
    I'll never say it!

CATHERINE:
    If you let love in, you'll get hurt. That's what
    happens.

MARGARET:
    You said a heart could block four shovels.

CATHERINE:
    I was wrong. The spades overtake the hearts,
    Margie. They always do. Think about it Margie! I'm
    warning you.

MARGARET rolls over in bed, her back to her mother.

MARGARET:
I'll think about it.

Scene Eight

Time passes. The men are into hard drinking.

NEIL:

> Nothing left. Nothing. Only thing you can do
> different from a pit pony is drink rum and play
> forty-five. 'Course you got your... *(IAN is embarrassed)*
> Come on. I've seen you down there in the sand dunes
> necking with Peggy. Nothing to be ashamed of.

IAN:

> *(drunk)* You go to hell. Why don't you get the hell
> out of here and go to mass.

NEIL:

> I might just do that. I'd rather listen to the music
> than your drunken ramblings... and pray for your
> soul at the same time.

IAN:

> My soul's alright. It's got a union card.

> *NEIL spits his drink out.*

NEIL:

> And you think that'll protect you, you idiot.

IAN:

> I'll put more faith in it than your bloody bagpipes.
> You're nothing but a freak Neil Currie. You're not a
> farmer, you're not a miner. You can't do nothing
> but make a whole lot of noise.

NEIL:

> Unless you know your history and your music, you
> don't know that the way things are is not necessarily
> the way things have to be.

76

IAN:

That's why we need a union.

NEIL:

That's why you need to know where ya came from.
You got roots deeper that those pits; you weren't
born into them, you were born to beautiful rolling
fields. We were farmers and we were sailors...

IAN:

And you're a pain in the arse.

NEIL:

You don't understand what I'm talking about.

IAN:

And that's the God's truth for you, Neil. Now why
don't you go on the couch and have a lay down.

NEIL stumbles to the couch and lies down.

NEIL:

I have one final question for you John.

IAN:

What is it?

NEIL:

Why were you kissing that mouse?

IAN:

I wasn't kissing it. I was counting its teeth and that's
the God's truth.

NEIL:

That's a good story John. You stick to it.

Scene Nine

*NEIL is standing looking out at the ocean. The
sound of seagulls screaming, wind, water.
MARGARET joins him.*

NEIL:
> I have your song for you, Mariead. The song about
> your brother. Would you like to hear it?

MARGARET:
> Is it in English? Will I understand it?

NEIL:
> I think so.

MARGARET:
> Alright then. Sing it.

NEIL:
> *(sings)* My brother was a miner.
> His name was Charlie David,
> He spent his young life laughing,
> And digging out his grave.
> *(chorus:)*
> Charlie Dave was big
> Charlie Dave was strong,
> Charlie Dave was two feet wide
> And almost six feet long.
>
> When Charlie David was sixteen
> He learned to chew and spit
> And went one day with Grandpa
> To work down in the pit
> *(chorus)*

When Charlie David was sixteen
He met his Maggie June
One day shift week they met at eight
On back shift week at noon.
  (chorus)
When Charlie David was sixteen
He said to June "Let's wed"
Maggie June was so surprised
She fell right out of bed
  (chorus)
When Charlie David was sixteen
They had a little boy
Maggie June was not surprised
Charlie danced for joy.
  (chorus)
When Charlie David was sixteen
The roof fell on his head
His laughing mouth is full of coal
Charlie Dave is dead.
  (chorus)

There is silence.

NEIL:

Margaret?

MARGARET:

(sniffling) It's lovely. It's almost as lovely as Charlie
Dave himself.

NEIL:

Good. Then it's settled. Let's lay him to rest. We've
talked enough about death. Let's get on with our life.

MARGARET:

Alright.

NEIL:
Do you like it here?

MARGARET:
I love it. I could stay here forever.

NEIL:
Then you will.

MARGARET:
What?

NEIL:
This land right here that we're standing on, I bought this yesterday with the pittance I got when I left the army. I'm going to build you a house, right here on the cliff, with the ocean boiling and spuming below. What do you think?

MARGARET:
I think that I'm ready Neil Currie!

NEIL lets out a shriek of happiness, He grabs her and twirls her around, then they kiss. Then he lets go of her and stamps his feet on the ground.

NEIL:
Right here Margaret! We're going to make our stand right here!

The light changes on MARGARET. NEIL moves away and she is back in the present.

MARGARET:
Right here.

Blackout

END OF ACT ONE

ACT TWO
Scene One

MARGARET is standing in her house, amongst her artifacts. She holds up a handful of notebooks.

MARGARET:
(reads) "This won't be written great for I am written it most in English for fear none will be able to read it in the Gallick for I can see how things are going." These are my great grandmother's scribblers. I finally found the time to read them... the ones I used for hotplates and fly swatters. Morag MacKinnon. Mabou-born and raised. Left with her Donald and the fiddlers and the pipers and the dancers, any that could walk at all and sober. Took the music with them and went to take jobs in the mines. It sounds like she was an awful terror. One day, when she came into the kitchen, the men were drinking and talking about giving up the only land they had left so they could make more money in the mines. So she grabbed the bottle and poured it into the slop pail with the morning piss. And they just sat there like gawks watching as she slapped the whole thing down on the table, piss splashing all over—"If you want to make pigs of yourself, here's the clear thing for it." Guts I'd say that took. Delicious guts. Morag. My mother's father's mother. Always raging. I vowed if I could even be half as lively as her...

Lights up on The Shack. NEIL is pouring over a pile of scribblers. CATHERINE is stepping around him cleaning. GRANDPA is napping. MARGARET walks in with a basket of vegetables from the garden, throws it all over the area which CATHERINE just cleared.

MARGARET:
 Turnips for dinner!

CATHERINE:
 I just wiped that!

MARGARET:
 Why'd you bother?

CATHERINE:
 Because I don't like living in a pigsty.

MARGARET:
 There are no pigs here mother. I wish there were.
 We could use a ham right now.

NEIL:
 (holds up a notebook) Read this Margaret.

MARGARET:
 I don't have time. I've got to make dinner... for my
 husband!

CATHERINE:
 Why don't you take some of your husband's clutter
 into your husband's bedroom.

MARGARET:
 Sure!

NEIL:

Then listen to this. *(reads)* "The silly arses, they think the job is like the land, that it just stays there. They're all too stunned to know that the job is like the music—it's like water in the woods. It's only there 'til it's gone. Show up one day for work and the washhouse door is locked." Now that's the truth. The truth lies there.

CATHERINE:

Well move it please 'cause I want to set the table.

NEIL:

70 years ago, your great grandmother knew that. And it's still the truth today.

CATHERINE:

It may be the truth but it's the job that puts the food on the table, not that pitiful excuse for a garden out there, nor that pile of scribblers that you pour over all day.

NEIL:

That's short thinking Catherine.

CATHERINE:

That's realistic thinking. Just one turnip each Margie. Those have to stretch a long way now that we've got one more mouth to feed—and a large one at that!

MARGARET comes over and kisses NEIL.

MARGARET:

There's more where that one came from.

NEIL:

> *(to CATHERINE)* Morag MacNeil had ten children living in a space not much bigger than this.

CATHERINE:

> And I should get comfort from that?

NEIL:

> Well, maybe encouragement and maybe even courage.

CATHERINE:

> Well I don't.

MARGARET:

> Sit down mom and take a load off your feet.

> *CATHERINE picks up the newspaper, scans the front page.*

CATHERINE:

> There are no jobs on the entire island it says here. Why put that in that paper? That's not news. We all know that. And I see we've just elected a CCF'er to Parliament. A socialist. Where are our heads? *(she throws the paper aside)* The papers just put me in a foul mood.

MARGARET:

> Well we don't want that.

> *CATHERINE takes a letter from her apron pocket.*

CATHERINE:

> The time has finally come to read my letter from your father's second cousin Roddie in Boston. I've let it age a couple of months. I guess I might as well get to it. See if there's any pressing news.

CATHERINE opens the letter, reads.

CATHERINE:
"Dear Catherine; Has it really been a year since last we corresponded?"

MARGARET:
That's how he starts every letter.

CATHERINE:
Thank heavens it has. *(reads)* "I trust you are all as well as can be expected." Given what he considers the pitiful state of our lives, but instead... "given the uncertain nature of modern life."

MARGARET:
What in God's earth is uncertain about putting buckles on patent-leather shoes all day?

CATHERINE:
"And that you are managing as well as can be expected since your terrible loss."

MARGARET:
Why doesn't he ever say their names?

CATHERINE:
"We've been blessed with another good year." Here they come....all their biggers and brand news. "We bought a brand new car to replace our old one which you may remember was a Ford Ambassador which we drove up to the funeral."

MARGARET:
We crammed every kid in the village in to it while he wasn't looking.

CATHERINE:
> I remember him turning up his nose at every car
> that came up the road. "Now how old is that 'ka'
> anyways?"

MARGARET:
> And old Sadie Gillis would answer with a smirk, "Oh
> well, she's old enough now, isn't she? She certainly
> isssss." That's the way the old Scotchy people talked.

CATHERINE:
> She sort of hissed like a tiny snake. *(reads on)* "This
> one has a bigger engine and a bigger wheelbase and
> a bigger glove compartment and a bigger steering
> wheel..."

NEIL:
> Sounds to me like he wishes he had a bigger...

> *MARGARET slaps him with a towel, he grabs her,*
> *pulls her down.*

CATHERINE:
> "...and a bigger seating capacity to meet the needs
> of our growing family."

> *CATHERINE looks over at MARGARET and NEIL*
> *horsing around.*

CATHERINE:
> Well bully for you Roddie.

MARGARET:
> What else does he say?

CATHERINE:
> *(reads on)* "And although I resisted as long as I
> could, Betty finally got her way with a brand new

bathroom, brand new sink, brand new flooring, brand new bathtub and most important of all, a spanking bright brand new toilet, which sits on what can only be described as a bit of a pedestal in the middle of the room."

NEIL:
God's teeth.

MARGARET giggles.

CATHERINE:
"Betty absolutely loves it."

MARGARET:
She's in love with a toilet.

NEIL:
Maybe she's never sat on anything else.

MARGARET giggles.

CATHERINE:
Don't knock a toilet Margie. It's nothing to snicker at.

CATHERINE throws the letter aside.

CATHERINE:
I'm not even going to finish it. It just makes me... sour. I don't want to hear another word.

MARGARET:
Oh come on mom.

NEIL:
There have always been people like that—they're little inside so they have to talk big.

CATHERINE:
   Still.

MARGARET:
   Finish it. He went to the trouble to write it. The least you can do is finish it.

CATHERINE:
   I don't want to.

MARGARET:
   Then I'll finish it. *(she takes the letter from CATHERINE, continues reading)* "We were delighted to hear that your sweet young daughter Margaret finally found a man to marry and regret that we could not make it to the wedding."

CATHERINE:
   Not that anyone asked you.

MARGARET:
   "We know how you have struggled and suffered over the years and hope that things will now look up for you with another breadwinner in the family. That's all for now. I'll write again soon."

   MARGARET puts the letter down. The mood has changed. She too looks subdued.

MARGARET:
   What an arse.

CATHERINE:
   What does he know about struggling and suffering?

   NEIL starts tuning his bagpipes.

MARGARET:
Do you have to do that now?

NEIL:
Yes, I do.

MARGARET:
(short) Well do it in the shed or the outhouse.

NEIL:
I will not.

MARGARET:
Sometimes I feel I married the both of you.

NEIL:
Well better than me and a toilet.

MARGARET:
I don't know. I'm sure a toilet brings some joy.

> *IAN walks in, stooped, exhausted, silent. He sits
> down, exhausted, stunned, black. They all watch him.*

NEIL:
Up from the deep for another whiff of air.

> *NEIL hands him the flask of rum, he takes a swig,
> closes his eyes.*

NEIL:
Can't your union do anything about all that soot
John that lands on your clothes?

IAN:
I'm not in the mood for your cracks tonight.

NEIL:
    Why not?

MARGARET:
    (teasing) Did Peggy stand you up before your shift?

    IAN doesn't answer.

CATHERINE:
    What is it?

IAN:
    We're all getting cut back two shifts a week.

CATHERINE:
    They can't do that.

    NEIL lets out another loud discordant blast on the pipes.

IAN:
    They're doing it.

CATHERINE:
    We can't pay the bills now.

    MARGARET reaches into the pot and takes out two potatoes.

MARGARET:
    We'll manage.

IAN:
    MacDougall says they don't need as much coal now that the war is over. Factories aren't producing.

NEIL:
    That's the truth. Don't need to make as many bombs to kill people.

IAN:

So they're squeezing the wages down.

NEIL:

The bastards! "Show up for work one day and the washhouse door is locked."

IAN:

I've got a union meeting tonight. We have to talk about strategy.

MARGARET:

(repeats) We'll manage. We always do. I've got a story. Did you hear about Johnny and Angie loading in 24, the roof so low they had to take pancakes in their cans?

NEIL continues to tune his bagpipes.

CATHERINE:

Outside with that.

NEIL:

I'm tuning it for the Ceilidh tonight.

CATHERINE:

Well that'll do us a lot of good. More money for rum.

MARGARET:

Mother!

CATHERINE:

Well?

NEIL:

It will bring in a little. As much as they can pay.

CATHERINE:
Milk money. Maybe. What's the value in that?

NEIL:
It will bring a smile and a tear and a memory to the people listening Catherine, and I can only hope there is value to that in heaven.

CATHERINE:
Oh for God's sake! What's that worth?

MARGARET:
He works whenever he can. He's travelled from one end of this island to the other to find work. But there is none. Even the paper says it. Half the island is on relief!

CATHERINE:
Well why isn't he on relief? He's fought for it. That's the least they can do for him. If it wasn't for his goddamned pride...

NEIL:
I won't take relief.

MARGARET:
(jumps in) Why don't you play that tune about the two hens fighting over a bean. Cheer us up.

CATHERINE:
I don't want to hear any more of that noise in this house. It gets in the way. We can't afford to be singing and dancing.

GRANDPA thumps his shoe in disapproval.

CATHERINE:

Don't try to shut me up. Someone's got to say what needs to be said. You've all gone off half-cocked. Look at poor Ian sitting there, half dead from exhaustion. He's been working underground since he was 15 years old. He's already stooped over from feeding us. And he doesn't have his own room anymore. Look at him. He never talks, he never says what's on his mind unless he's got two sheets to the wind and then it's all just union nonsense.

MARGARET:

Stop it mom.

CATHERINE:

Speak up Ian. What have you got to say about that?

IAN:

How about some peace and quiet?

CATHERINE:

Speak up for yourself Ian. How can you not mind? Three men in the house, one can't talk or won't, the other can't stop talking or squawking. Three men, one pay. What do you think of that.

They all look to IAN. MARGARET holds her breath.

IAN:

I don't mind mom.

CATHERINE:

Why not?

IAN:

Because that's the way he sees it. You've got to
believe in something. I believe in the union but I
gotta admit we're not making much headway right
now. I'm not sure what he believes in but he sure as
hell believes it hard. *(turns to NEIL)* Hey, I forgot to
tell you. I saw a truck pull up at the Co-op. They
might be looking for a hand.

*NEIL gets up quickly and leaves. MARGARET looks
over at her brother with love in her eyes.*

Scene Two

*Night. NEIL comes stumbling in, good and drunk,
singing. MARGARET is sleeping. She hears him
stumbling in, gets up and helps him.*

MARGARET:
   Shhhh... You drunken fool! Shhhh...

NEIL:
   Don't shush me up Margaret.

MARGARET:
   I will. Or you'll wake everyone.

NEIL:
   Well wake 'em all and let's have a party.

MARGARET:
   Get your boots off. Get to bed.

NEIL:
   Do you love me Mairead?

MARGARET:
   A little. Get your boots off.

NEIL:
   D'you wish you had a toilet to sit on and a great big
   car.

MARGARET:
   Don't be foolish.

NEIL:
   I can't give you those things.

MARGARET:

    That's not what I want.

NEIL:

    I want to give you a house by the ocean cause you're a little seadog... I can tell. That's where you want your nose... sniffing the salt air.

MARGARET:

    And you will. We'll build that house.

NEIL:

    Where's the pride Mairead?

MARGARET:

    What?

NEIL:

    Where's the pride?

MARGARET:

    Shut your yap and go to sleep

NEIL:

    Know what I did tonight from one 'til four in the morning?

MARGARET:

    No, but I guess I'm gonna hear about it.

NEIL:

    I unpacked a whole truck to get the six boxes of supplies going to the Glace Bay Co-op, then I loaded it up again. Then 'cause some goddamn idiot had forgotten about two pitiful boxes of toilet paper at the very back I unloaded it all again. And I got yelled at for that by a mean-mouthed excuse of a man 'cause I wasn't working fast enough. And I wanted to pound him but I didn't 'cause I needed the two dollars. Where's the pride? There's got to be pride in the work just like there's pride in the music. That's one thing you can say about Ian. He's got a man's job. He knows he's not a worm even though he is worming around in the ground. The money is in the pit.

MARGARET:

Oh shut up. You made two bucks. That'll buy food and shingles. Stop feeling sorry for yourself.

NEIL:

Maybe he's right. Maybe I am some kind of a freak who just makes noise.

MARGARET:

(strokes his hair) Go to sleep.

> *NEIL starts to snore. MARGARET pulls herself out from under NEIL's weight, then stands up.*

MARGARET:

(to audience) But it wasn't always like that. There were times away from the shack when we'd get down to the water. We'd start at one end of the beach, the Dominion side and walk along the breaking waves in our bare feet across to the Lingan side and cross the bridge there and sometimes we'd find Ian and Peggy sneaking some time together and we'd throw sand on top of them then haul them along with us but more often it would just be Ian who'd come so they could get in a bit more squabbling time and if lobster was in season, we'd buy some and borrow a pot from a fisherman and cook 'em up and eat them right there and drink beer... God, you talk about good.

97

NEIL:

Your union's got about as much clout as a wet mop in a rainstorm.

IAN:

I got an idea. How 'bout we start a farm in the backyard. We got at least fifty square feet, we'll grow all our own vegetables, and keep a cow and a pig and a couple of beef cattle and some chickens and for money to buy beer and pay the light bill, we'll rent you and your pipes out to concerts!

NEIL:

I like the sound of that!

The sound of people yelling. They all stop, look at something ahead, their eyes wide.

NEIL:

There's something happening up ahead.

MARGARET:

(to audience) There was a whale stranded half on shore and half in the water and there were two fishing boats straining with all their might to tug it out to sea with ropes. And there was a bunch of drunken galoots on top of the poor brute, dancing on it, trying to punch holes in its sides.

IAN:

Look what those bastards are doing!

NEIL holds onto IAN's arm.

NEIL:

It's too late to help. The whale's dead.

IAN:

You don't know that.

NEIL:

Look at it!

IAN:

Let me go!

NEIL:

There's gotta be ten of them, you silly bugger! You can't beat your way through that bunch.

IAN:

Well I'm gonna try.

IAN breaks free. NEIL has no choice but to follow.

MARGARET:

(to audience) I watched them run down the beach and then wade into the middle of those bloody brawling fools. I don't think even Charlie Dave could of made a dent in that bunch. There were arms and fists and feet and oaths flying 'til the air was black and blue but maybe it satisfied the bullies bloodlust because after they finished beating the pulp out of Ian and Neil, they gave up on the poor stranded beast and left it alone. Then the Mounties came—too late as usual—and everyone hurried off so they wouldn't be part of a police report. That is everyone but the whale who was still waiting for high tide.

NEIL and IAN enter, bloody but walking.

IAN:

You alright?

NEIL:
Yeah. You?

IAN:
Yeah.

NEIL:
You goddamn idiot. I should have let you kill
yourself.

IAN:
Well then why didn't you?

NEIL:
I got my pride eh.

IAN:
Well Jesus Neil, didn't you see what they were
doing?

NEIL:
I'm not blind. I saw what was going on but it wasn't
our business.

IAN:
How would you like someone spittin' in your face?

NEIL:
For Christ sake Ian, it's only a goddamned whale.

IAN:
Sure it's only a goddamned whale and I'm only a
goddamned coal miner.

NEIL:
What's that supposed to mean?

IAN:

It was just trying to save its life and when it needed
a bit of help, a bunch of bullies come along and try
punching holes in it, spit on it and piss all over it.
You gotta help out. We knocked them off at least
didn't we?

NEIL:

Just about killed ourselves

IAN:

But we didn't, did we?

NEIL:

The friggin thing's had it. Look at him. He's not
going anywhere.

IAN:

You don't know that for sure. You don't know what
it's made of, what kind of will it's got to live... or
how strong those fishermen's lines are. If the
fishermen can pull him off with their ropes when
the tide comes in, who knows, it might have a
chance yet. Those bastards spit in its face but that
whale's still got pride.

NEIL:

A friggin whale's pride.

IAN:

Yeh. A friggin whale's pride. It's struggling along
too eh, just like the rest of us. You just can't give up.
You can't just sit by. We helped him out and maybe
now he's got a chance.

NEIL:

Maybe he does and maybe he doesn't.

IAN:

Well one thing I know for sure—if you don't work at it, if you don't fight for it, it ain't gonna happen. That's what the union's all about.

NEIL:

Well maybe you're right about the union... but the best thing would be if you didn't work in the pit at all.

IAN:

The thing of it, Mr. Know-It-All-Neil Currie... what did you say? Did you say that I'm right about union?

NEIL:

Yes, I did say that Ian.

IAN:

Well wonder of wonders. And you called me Ian.

NEIL:

Yes, I did.

IAN:

Well God Almighty.

NEIL:

I guess you spent so much time nosing through the earth you wore your nose down short and now you can see beyond the end of it.

IAN:

I can?

NEIL:

Yep. You got a good head, you got a brave heart and you got a short nose, and your great grandmother Morag would've been proud of you. She was all in favour of people whose eyes are longer than their noses.

IAN seems to grow taller as NEIL talks.

IAN:

Say that again—about being right about the union.

NEIL:

But she wasn't crazy about the rum bottle. She'd a thought piss would've been a better drink for the likes of us!

IAN:

Come on, say it again.

NEIL:

Oh for God's sakes.

IAN:

Just say that part about me being right about the union.

NEIL:

Give it up.

IAN:

Just say it. Slowly.

NEIL:

You're right about the union,

IAN lets out a 'Yip' of delight and the two of them walk off wrestling.

Scene Three

The Shack. A month later. GRANDPA is methodically lifting a pair of soup cans up and down, trying to build his muscles. He starts to wheeze and cough. NEIL enters, comes over and gives him his thump. GRANDPA's breathing improves.

NEIL:
> Better not overdo it gramps.

> *NEIL sits down heavily and starts carving a piece of wood. GRANDPA scribbles something in his notebook and hands it to NEIL.*

NEIL:
> *(reads)* "Call the undertaker. Neil Currie's passed away."

> *NEIL laughs.*

NEIL:
> Do I look that bad?

> *GRANDPA nods.*

NEIL;
> I'm sorry. I'm not very good company for you.

> *GRANDPA writes something.*

NEIL:
> *(reads)* "I'm no hell either."

> *NEIL looks at GRANDPA, laughs.*

NEIL:

At least I don't have to fight to get a word in edgewise. *(NEIL studies the old man)* Why did you stop talking?

GRANDPA stares off.

NEIL:

Would you like me to sing you something?

GRANDPA nods. NEIL starts singing 'The Isle of Skye.' While he does this, GRANDPA writes something in his notebook. By the time NEIL finishes, GRANDPA has nodded off to sleep. NEIL takes the notebook and reads it.

NEIL:

(reads) "The doctors said there was nothing wrong with my lungs. He was a liar. But no one wanted to hear what I had to say." *(to the sleeping man)* So you stopped talking. Nobody wants to hear what I have to say either. I sleep in my wife's mother's shack and I hardly make enough to buy the tea.

NEIL puts a blanket over GRANDPA's chest.

NEIL:

Well at least I take care of you. I give you your thump every hour.

NEIL gets out his flask, takes a drink, goes back to woodworking. MARGARET and CATHERINE and IAN enter. The women are tired, they drop their bags. MARGARET looks over at NEIL, he keeps his head down. There are two pillows lying on a kitchen chair. CATHERINE stares at them, then moves them out of the way.

CATHERINE:
> Well, it's good to be home. To the things I'm used to. When I work up at the MacDougall's or the MacGregor's I miss the pillows on the kitchen chairs. I miss the underwear draped over my one decent sitting chair.

> *MARGARET tries to find a place for the pillows and her underwear. She is sick of her mother's cracks. She looks over at NEIL, who is ignoring her.*

CATHERINE:
> I see we've got a new leak in the roof. Oh well, I guess I should be glad I've got a roof over my head at all these days. Wipe your nose, Margie, it's dripping like a tap.

> *MARGARET takes out a handkerchief and wipes it.*

CATHERINE:
> You peel the potatoes. And try not to whittle them down to nothing like you did last night. And don't boil the daylights out of them either. I'll try to squeeze another meal out of this scrawny little chicken for the five of us.

> *MARGARET gets out some potatoes, starts slamming them into the pot. IAN drops his stuff. He opens a little bag and pulls out a new tie. He examines it proudly. Then he pulls out some paper, sits down at the kitchen table, starts writing.*

CATHERINE:
> And what's all this?

IAN:

I'm working on a talk I'm gonna give at the union
hall tonight. I'm the new secretary treasurer for
District 26.

CATHERINE:

Will that bring more money into the house?

IAN:

It's not a paying position mom. It's an honour.

CATHERINE:

Oh. *(to MARGARET)* Don't leave the lid off of the
oil. I can never find it.

IAN:

Did you know that the old Sydney and Dominion
collieries pay two completely different wage scales
for exactly the same kind of operation?

CATHERINE:

Which is lower?

IAN:

Ours.

CATHERINE:

Figures.

IAN:

And that the contract mining rates are 7% lower
than they were in '26 in terms of real money.

CATHERINE:

There was no money anywhere in '26. Just turnips
and weak tea. Don't talk to me about '26.

CATHERINE takes exception to the new location
where MARGARET has put the pillows and blanket.

CATHERINE:
And don't leave them there! I'll just trip over them
on my way to the outhouse.

MARGARET:
Well where should I put it? Should I hang it from
the roof?

CATHERINE:
Could you? That might help.

MARGARET:
(short) No, I can not!

IAN:
We want a pension plan for all miners over 65. Only
a quarter of them get any kind of pension at all and
that just depends on whether you sucked up to the
company enough.

CATHERINE:
(looks over at GRANDPA) He sure didn't and look
what he got. Nothing! They didn't even give him
the time of day.

IAN:

And we want to get rid of the company doctors
'cause they just say what the company wants to hear.

NEIL looks up and over at the sleeping old man then
back down at his carving. NEIL takes another drink
from his flask. MARGARET watches him, steaming.

CATHERINE:

Speaking of the doctor, I cleaned over there today. She's got shelves for this and shelves for that... If Charlie Dave were here—

MARGARET:

(sharp) Well he's not.

CATHERINE:

(taken aback) Well I know he's not. I was just going to say that if he were, he'd be able to rig up some kind of shelves to put all that stuff on. I don't know where he got so handy. He sure didn't get it from his father and he sure didn't pass it along to his brother. Now if I had a kitchen like that—

MARGARET:

Well you don't!

CATHERINE:

I know I don't. What's wrong with you today?

MARGARET shakes her head.

IAN:

Now all I need to do is get everyone talking about this stuff. There's a lot of them have their noses so close to the rock face, they can't see for nothing.

MARGARET tries to stuff the pillows into a drawer. CATHERINE picks up some clothes.

CATHERINE:

And while you're at it, could you get these out of sight.

MARGARET:

No, I cannot! There is nowhere to put it.

CATHERINE:
Don't pout. You're not ten years old.

MARGARET:
That's right. I am not ten years old. I am a grown woman. A married woman. I don't have to listen to my mother bossing me around from dawn 'til dusk!

NEIL:
(looks up) Steady Margaret.

MARGARET:
No, I won't be steady! All you do is sit around and drink all day and play those damn things. I'm sick of it! I don't want to live here any more. I want to be on our own land. I want to live with my husband in my own place. Where's my house?

MARGARET storms out. CATHERINE goes into the other room. GRANDPA nods off to sleep. NEIL and IAN start playing cards.

IAN:

There's a job opened up in No. 10. I could get you in.

NEIL says nothing.

IAN:

Whatdiya say?

NEIL says nothing.

IAN:

What happened to you that day down there when you were roaring around like a stuck bull?

NEIL:

I've told you what I think about the pit and it's the God's truth.

IAN:

I know it is... but I wanna know about that day.

NEIL:

(after a pause) I was down there a mile below the earth digging away at the coal face trying not to think about where I was and what I was doing... and then all of a sudden my light went out. Ever happen to you?

IAN:

Yeah.

NEIL:

I was scared shitless. I never be so scared in my life—not over there in the war, not anywhere. And then this song came into my head, something I'd heard the old people sing, in Gaelic, and it started pouring out of me, and it kept getting louder and louder. And the foreman came roaring up and told me to shut up but I wouldn't, I couldn't. And maybe everyone thought I was crazy but it helped me. It was like a light guiding me. As soon as we got back up top, I quit, just a second before he fired me. *(long pause)* You ever get scared down there?

IAN:

Christ, all the time.

NEIL:

You do?

IAN:

Margaret used to have to walk me to work back shift when I started cause I was so scared of the dark. *(laughs)* That was one of the reasons I started going with girls.... I couldn't have my sister walking to me work forever.

NEIL:

Well I'll be damned.

IAN:

I don't know this for sure, but maybe everyone feels the same way. I could use some help for a while Neil. You could work right beside me. The union needs good men.

NEIL throws the cards down on the table. The lights go down.

Scene Four

The ocean. MARGARET is on their land. NEIL joins her.

MARGARET:

I'm sorry I said those things.

NEIL:

What you said cleared the air. *(looking out)* You know Mairead, if it weren't for that bit of water out there, you could walk right up on the shore of the Isle of Skye. *(after a pause)* I'm going to go underground and help Ian. I'll be a miner until I can put a roof over our head and a down payment on ten sheep.

He kisses her.

Scene Five

The Shack. MARGARET is reading the paper.
CATHERINE is cleaning. GRANDPA is napping
with a couple of soup cans lying in his lap.
CATHERINE looks at GRANDPA.

CATHERINE:
Well I think I'll take these back Mr. Charles Atlas if
you don't mind.

CATHERINE tries to ease the soup cans out of
GRANDPA's lap and he wakes up, grabs hold of the
soup cans and starts lifting them up and down.
CATHERINE watches him, smiles, rubs his shoulder
affectionately.

CATHERINE:
Maybe I'll get my shelves built yet!

MARGARET:
(reading from paper) "This is the first time since 1917
the miners have entered wage negotiations armed
with a strike mandate." *(looks up)* I wish I was at that
strike meeting.

CATHERINE:
I wish I was at bingo. At least there I have a hope in
hell of winning.

IAN and NEIL enter. MARGARET, CATHERINE
and GRANDPA all look expectant.

MARGARET:
Well?

NEIL:

Well, I thought the union head made pretty good sense. We could sure use $2.50 more a day. It would get me out of that hole faster. I think it's time to bust their asses.

MARGARET:

That's 'cause you love a fight!

NEIL:

(turns to IAN) What do you think? You've been pretty quiet all the way home. Cat got your tongue?

IAN:

(cautious) We'd need somebody to talk to the women, to explain how much better off we'd be if we stick together.

NEIL:

Margaret can do that. Maybe get Peggy to help you. *(laughs)* That would be a sight wouldn't it? The mine manager's daughter organizing the miners' wives!

MARGARET:

You think I'm gonna talk to every coal miner's wife in Reserve?

IAN:

No, it would have to be all the collieries. We'd have to get the wives from every colliery backing their men.

MARGARET:

I'd do it, but I don't know how.

CATHERINE:

>You're all talking like it's a picnic you're organizing. It's not. A strike is hell. I know. *(nods to GRANDPA)* So does he.

NEIL:

>Do you think we can get all the collieries?

IAN:

>I think we can. All of them in District 26.

NEIL:

>But you're nervous, aren't ya? What is it?

IAN:

>I asked Peggy to sound out her father on a strike.

NEIL:

>Well I guess we know what he'd say.

IAN:

>He used to be a miner. He's not a bad guy. He might be telling the truth.

NEIL:

>So what did he tell her?

IAN:

>That hell would freeze over before the company would touch its profits.... and in the meantime, the miners' families could starve...

CATHERINE:

>And they will.

NEIL:

>But the UMW will back us up. They said so.

116

IAN:

MacDougall says they say they will—but they won't.

NEIL:

How the hell does he know that?

IAN:

In the last election, the miners elected a socialist to the federal government. The UMW is an American union. To an American, a socialist is a communist. The union can't be seen in the States as supporting communism. As soon as word gets out that the Glace Bay miners are a bunch of communists, the American union leaders will drop us like a hot potato.

CATHERINE:

Well that settles it. Forget the whole thing.

NEIL:

Is that all?

IAN:

MacDougall said there are some good jobs coming up. Jobs he thought the two of us would be just right for. Surface jobs. The pay's good and good chance for advancement. But if we were seen as instigators of the strike, we wouldn't have a hope in hell of getting them after the dust settled.

NEIL:

The bastard's trying to buy us off.

CATHERINE:

Take them. For God's sake, take the jobs. Forget the strike. MacDougall's already said that the decks stacked against you.

NEIL:

We don't know if he's right. He may be just trying to spook us.

IAN:

Is that what you think Neil?

CATHERINE:

Why don't you ask what I think? If you're so interested in stories, why don't you ask what I think?!

NEIL:

What do you think Catherine?

CATHERINE:

I remember standing on the hill above Lingan beach with my three children—Margaret was in my arms, watching my own grandfather and my father and my husband and 3000 miners take a strike vote in front of a bonfire. They were so full of themselves, so sure that they were right, that they would win. But they didn't.

IAN:

But they were right.

CATHERINE:

I remember no food and filthy water and children dying of disease 'cause our water was filthy. I remember company thugs setting fires to our houses and police running over people with their horses...and in the end, they only got back a fraction of what they'd lost. And now, I have one less son and a dead husband and an old man who's lost his voice. You can't win against them.

They are all silent.

IAN:
> There's another thing.

NEIL:
> What's that?

IAN:
> Peggy said if we go on strike, I shouldn't count on
> her being there when it's over.

MARGARET:
> That's low.

> *NEIL turns to GRANDPA.*

NEIL:
> What do you think Grandpa? If you were still in the
> pit what would you do?

> *Everyone waits. GRANDPA finally scribbles a note,*
> *pushes it towards NEIL.*

NEIL:
> *(reads)* "I'd fight again. If you don't fight for what
> you believe, you are a worm!"

MARGARET:
> *(to the audience)* I helped out during the strike.
> People who wouldn't even give me the time of day
> when I walked by welcomed me into their homes
> cause I was Ian's sister or I was Neil Currie's wife.
> And a lot of the older ones even remembered the
> role my great grandmother Morag played in the last
> great strike hauling endless stores of vegetables
> which she'd wrapped in paper in her cellar and
> giving them to the children in exchange for their
> learning some Gaelic. Being Morag MacNeil's great
> granddaughter, I had about as much roots as a

scraggly little bush could have in this God-forsaken
windy place.

MARGARET is remembering music.

MARGARET:
And 'cause nobody was working, all the singers and
fiddlers and dancers had time on their hands and
they'd go around giving free concerts, or they'd
charge a little and give the money to the relief fund.
Neil was in seventh heaven. This was what life was
supposed to be. But the best thing of all about the
strike was that it gave Neil time to finish the house.

NEIL:
Here is it Mairead. Your house on the ocean. This is
where we'll make our stand.

*NEIL watches MARGARET takes a deep breath, then
she lets out a triumphant whoop.*

NEIL:
You're like a perfectly tuned set of pipes You always
make the right sound. It comes from deep inside
you. You'll be alright Mairead. You'll always do the
right thing. I love you Margaret MacNeil.

MARGARET:
I love you Neil Currie.

He kisses her. NEIL moves off.

MARGARET:
(to audience) Of course everything MacDougall said
came true. Once the strike got going, it seemed to
drop out of the hands of the miners completely.
The big meetings all took place in Montreal.
Nobody knew what was going on, but when it finally

ended, we were no better off than before. Instead of the $2.50 that we asked for, the union made a deal for a dollar a day I think it was but even that didn't amount to anything because they only got the raise if they put out more coal than before the strike, which was nearly impossible. But the worst of it was, if there hadn't been a strike and MacDougall kept his word, Ian and Neil might have been working on the surface instead of in the pit. As it were, they were both killed the same minute.

The sound of a mine whistle.

MARGARET:

I was up to Reserve keeping house for my mother when I heard the whistle. I heard the dogs howling for two nights before so soon's I heard the whistle, I took off for the pit. They were both just being taken up when I got there. They had them in the half ton truck with blankets over them. I told them to take them to my mother's where they lay one of them on mama's bed and one on the couch in the kitchen. Then I told them to get out. I knew what to get. I helped Charlie Dave keep a dead frog for two years when he was going to school. I went to the Medical Hall and got two gallons of the stuff. Cost me a lot. I got back as fast as I could, but it wasn't quick enough. I locked the house before I left so nobody could get in. Mama was visiting her sister in Bras d'Or and I didn't know when she'd be back. When I got back, there was a bunch around the door. I told them to fuck off. I was busy. To make matters worse my grandfather was left alone all that time. He died. He choked. But before he did, he wrote this—

MARGARET picks up a notebook.

MARGARET:

(reads) "It's kind of comical if it wasn't so sad,
there's our Margaret married to the only one you'd
think wouldn't work in the pit but there he is
working in it anyway and him working with Ian, if
the two of them get killed....what will the poor girl
do?

MARGARET looks up from the notebook.

MARGARET:

I took his lungs. It wasn't so much the lungs
themselves, though, I think they were a good thing
to take, though they don't keep too well, especially
the condition he was in, as just something to
remind me of the doctor who told him he couldn't
get compensation because he was fit to work. Then
I took Neil's lungs because I thought of them
connected to his pipes and they show, compared to
grandfather's, what lungs should look like. And I
took his tongue since he always said he was the only
one around still had one. I took his fingers too,
because he played the pipes with them. I didn't
know what to take from Ian so I took his dick since
Neil always said that was Ian's substitute for religion
to keep him from being a pit pony when he wasn't
drinking rum or playing forty-five. I had each thing
in its own pickle jar. I put them all in the tin
suitcase with the scribblers and the deck of cards
and the half empty quart of black death they left
after last Sunday's drinking and arguing, got Neil's
bagpipes and took it all over to my friend Marie's
next door for safe keeping. They came in a police
car and I didn't give them a chance to even get out
of the car. I jumped right into the back seat like it
was a taxi I was waiting for. I just sat right in and
said "Sydney River please." Sydney River, if you're
not from around here is the cookie jar where they

put rotten tomatoes so they won't spoil the barrel. So they put me in 'til they forgot about me; then when they remembered me they forgot what they put me in for. So they let me go.

MARGARET's House by the Ocean: MARGARET is standing looking out the window, suitcase on the floor beside her. CATHERINE enters. They look at each other.

MARGARET:
Hello mom.

CATHERINE:
(guarded) Hello, Margie.

MARGARET takes a deep breath.

MARGARET:
Oh the air smells like heaven here, doesn't it?

CATHERINE:
I guess.

MARGARET:
You look good. The house looks good. Thank you for keeping it so nice for me 'til I got back.

CATHERINE:
I didn't mind. It's a bit big for me though. Alone.

MARGARET:
You can stay here and live with me mother, if you like.

CATHERINE:
Thanks anyway. But I'm not feeling too good. I think I'll go back to Reserve.

MARGARET:
So stay. I'll look after you.

CATHERINE:
Yes, you'll look after me. You'll look after me. And what if I drop dead during the night?

MARGARET:
If you drop dead during the night, you're dead. Dead in Glace Bay is the same as being dead in Reserve.

CATHERINE:
Yes. And you'll look after me dead, too, I imagine. You'll look after me. What'll you do? Cut off my tits and put them in bottles.

MARGARET:
Mother, your tits don't mean a thing to me.

CATHERINE picks up her suitcase, opens the door and leaves.

MARGARET:
(calls after her) Have you got everything?

CATHERINE:
(calls back) If I've forgotten anything, pickle it.

MARGARET:
Okay.

CATHERINE:
Keep it for a souvenir!

MARGARET:
Okay!

MARGARET shuts the door.

MARGARET:
(*to audience*) I was sorry after that I said what I said. I wouldn't have minded having one of her tits. After all, if it wasn't for them, we'd have all died of thirst before we had our chance to get killed.

The strains of 'MacPherson's Lament' begin and grow throughout the rest of MARGARET's memories.

MARGARET:
Marie came over with the suitcase and we had a cup of tea and she helped me set things up. We had to make shelves for the jars. Everything else can go on tables and chairs or hang on the wall or from the ceiling as you can see. Marie is very artistic, she knows how to put things around. I'm the cook. We give tea and scones free to anyone who comes. You're the first. I guess not too many people know about it yet. But it will pick up. These things take time.

A light comes up on NEIL in memory.

NEIL:
I think you're the smallest son of a bitch I ever seen. I love you Margaret MacNeil.

A light comes up on CATHERINE.

CATHERINE:
That man will never live in a company house. And he can work with Ian. They can die together. And you can live in your shack alone. Stand it then.

Another light comes up on IAN.

IAN:

It's only a goddamned whale and I'm only a goddamned coal miner. But one thing I know for sure, if you don't work at it, if you don't fight for it, it ain't gonna happen.

MARGARET continues humming. Another light.

NEIL:

Go and read your grandfather's scribblers. He remembers. His blood was spilled there, on the ground, and our blood was spilled there, on the ground. He remembers.

MARGARET:

It's important to remember. Because we sort of are what we remember. And when you leave, take a walk out to the cliff. Take a good look.

Light on NEIL.

NEIL:

You know Mairead, if it wasn't for that bit of water out there, you could walk right up on the shore of the Isle of Skye. That's where we come from.

Bagpipes swell at the end.

MARGARET:

Just an ocean away. Just one good spit away.

THE END